Prophetic Poems

God Speaks to His People

Arlene Mary Thibault

Arlene Mary Thibault

PublishAmerica
Baltimore

©Copyright 2002 by Arlene Mary Thibault.

All rights reserved. No part of this book may be reproduced in any form without written permission from the publishers, except by a reviewer who may quote brief passages in a review to be printed in a newspaper or magazine.

First printing

ISBN: 1-59129-421-5
PUBLISHED BY PUBLISHAMERICA BOOK PUBLISHERS
www.publishamerica.com
Baltimore

Printed in the United States of America

~ *Dedication* ~

To God, who in a series of prayer times, enlivened my human spirit by His Holy Spirit inspiration to receive these words of His love in rhyme.

And to my husband, Ed, our family, and friends of Cornerstone Fellowship who have encouraged me, especially Lola Castro, Helen Martinek, and Minnie Thompson of the Thursday afternoon Simeon and Anna worship, word and sharing group.

John 10:27 "My sheep listen to my voice; I know them and they follow me."

Dear Readers, beloved of God,

For many years my husband and I shared God's love and the Gospel with the elderly in Nursing Homes. Now, we are elderly ourselves and with the new Revival outpouring of the Holy Spirit and the Father's Blessing we have become joyful worshipers, drawn ever closer to our Sovereign Lord Jesus.

In our seventies now, the Lord brings us into His realm of overcoming as we rise above Ed's cancer and my spinal difficulty requiring surgery.

Every day our gracious Lord shows us more of Himself as we worship and read His Holy Word. We have wonderful sharing conversations. Our lives are richly blessed.

I asked the Lord for generosity and He gave me poetry to share. May you be so intrigued by the words of the poems that you will read the Scripture reference* while praying the Revival prayer, "More, Lord, More!" May God bless each of you to know the height, breadth and depth of His love for you.

Love in Jesus' Spirit,
Arlene Mary Thibault

*Scripture references are from the NIV (New International Version) Bible.

TABLE OF CONTENTS

FORWARD - Prophetic Rhymes   9

I   PRAYER (Conversations with God):   11
Alpha & Omega; Zephaniah 3:17; Ponder My Words; I Am Teaching You; Pentecost Now; Gethsemane Cup; Signs & Wonders; The Father's Love; Chosen & Sent; Ephesians Praise; God is Life; Who Am I?; Gardens.

II   INTERCESSION: 27
There Is No Other; Jesus Praying; Prodigal Return; Cries & Tears; Alien, Stranger, Pilgrim; This Blessed Task; Royal Priesthood; Intercession For A City; Acts Today; I Read The Newspaper; Pedestrian.

III   WITNESSES: (Acts 1:8)   41
Each With A Story; Enoch; Faith Sees Hope; Mary; Simeon & Anna; Nicodemus; Grandmother Grace; Prophets; Freedom Song; Out Of The Box; Now Is The Day; Sons Of God Arise; These Two Commandments; Worship Meeting Plan; Traveling Song; Wonderful Lord; Servant Messengers.

IV   HEALING: 61
I Need Healing; Broken Temple; Hold Out Your Hand; That's Why I Ask; Thorn In My Side; Support Is A Stepping Stone; God's Embrace; The Word Among Us; Sovereign Love Wins; My Uncle Was Healed; Isaac's Wood; I Touched Him; These Are My People; Beyond Healing.

V HOPE IN GOD: 77
God Has Ascended; Father's Day; Firstborn Of Many Others; The Corner Of My Robe Is Over You; Hope Song; We Came; Greater Things; Basic Truth: You Are Beloved of God.

VI THERE'S "MORE": 89
Overview; Homecoming; Human Beings Asleep; Forgiven, Forgiving; Two Voices, Two Choices; Come to Me; You Also Will Live; My Treasure; Signs of Love; The King's Provision; Mercy; Zacchaeus; Obedient; Pearls from Pressure

EPILOGUE: For Posterity – My Poetry 105

FORWARD

PROPHETIC RHYMES

God, our Father, Lord of the Universe
    Doesn't always speak in verse,
But I asked Him for generosity
    And He gave me poetry.

To us sheep, Jesus also speaks prose;
    His ways are way above those
Of ours, so I've listened and tried
    To generously share the Sanctified.

My therapy worked, I'm feeling fine.
    Even in the kitchen I write a line.
God's Holy word heard before and read
    Runs through my head even in bed.

I know all doesn't need to be in rhyme
    But how short is my sharing lifetime:
Our Father, keeping it a surprise, knows
    He owns the mystery He chose.

May you know Jesus and find interest
    In reading His word daily to be blessed.
May you have "More!" of The Spirit Holy,
    Blessed by our Father eternally.

John 10:1-18
Matthew 24:36

I
PRAYER: CONVERSATIONS WITH GOD:

ALPHA AND OMEGA

ZEPHANIAH 3:17

PONDER MY WORDS

I AM TEACHING YOU

PENTECOST NOW

GETHSEMANE CUP

SIGNS AND WONDERS

THE FATHER'S LOVE

CHOSEN AND SENT

EPHESIANS PRAISE

GOD IS LIFE

WHO AM I?

GARDENS

ALPHA AND OMEGA

I AM Alpha and Omega, beginning and end.
    You know by The Holy Spirit I send,
That I AM, who was, who is, who is to come,
    First on earth to those of My Kingdom.

You are believers, My kingdom of priests
    By My sacrificed Blood of Love released
To worship in your body "Temple," serving
    God, Our Father, praise deserving.

I AM the "pierced One," for all to see,
    Each person mourning in humility,
To see My hands and feet that bore sin shame,
    Each repentant, longing for My Name.

O my God, I stand in breath-held awe!
    In Your word here, I never before saw
You've already begun to make all things new,
    Start with me; give me awesome new view!

Father in heaven, all praise to Your Name!
    Jesus, Bread of Life, destroying my shame!
Please forgive me more, as more I forgive,
    Deliver me victorious, in Your Spirit to live.

A.M.T., May 21, 1999

Revelation 1:6-8; Colossians 3:10
Matthew 6:9-15

ZEPHANIAH 3:17

I Am Lord God, mighty to save.
    Loving you first, My Son I gave.
I started the song to be a duet.
    I sing over you rejoicing. . .yet
My greatest joy of My song to invite,
    Is My Bride responding in delight.

Garments of righteousness for you My Bride,
    I AM Bridegroom, waiting for you to decide
To say "Yes!" Then, you can hear My song
    And wonder why you took so long
To answer Me, Lord of Lords and King
    Who wants you, Bride at His wedding!

My Bride, in loving joy, I delight in you
    And quiet you with My love true,
I rejoice over you with singing
    At this Banquet, in joy celebrating!
Sing with Me this joyful song;
    To My family you forever belong.

Holy Spirit, give Your Church, a melody
    Of praise and worship harmony
To God Our Father who gives us life,
    His Son, Jesus, desiring us as wife!
So we in love, begin worship, praising
    Him for love so amazing!

                A.M.T., April 1999

Zephaniah 3:17; Matthew 22:2;
Revelation 19:6-16

PONDER MY WORDS

I Am God, with words and actions to ponder
    To treasure in your heart in awed wonder
As simple believers, not like the worldly wise,
    Who examine and foolishly analyze.

My love for you is beauty in mystery;
    My word, My story is more than history
Revealing My care for you and for all,
    Before, and after the Fall.

You each ratified the sin of Adam and Eve.
    It took you a time to believe,
To repent, receiving My forgiveness,
    A time for you to become My witness.

You read and pondered My word,
    Knew it as a two-edged sword.
You came to the foot of My cross with Mary
    To find faith in circumstance contrary.

Ponder anew the blessings I have given.
    Remember now, preparing for heaven.
I knew you when you were seven and eleven,
    I AM with you at age seventy-seven.

Let your heart of worship begin anew,
    As you recount mercies I've given you.
Stay with me, let your aging be a pleasure,
    Counting Me as your life-long treasure.

A.M.T., May 3, 1999

Luke 2:19; Psalm 71;
1 Corinthians 1:18-30

I AM TEACHING YOU

I Myself Am reaching, teaching you,
    Many of you, not just a few.
I Am calling you together, to be first;
    Ready for those who will thirst.

There is to be a cresting wave
    Of seeking people who will crave
My Life, My Word, and My goodness,
    Escaping fruit of evil – sadness.

Be ready with Word and Worship song,
    Delighting The Father and Jesus, Son.
I Am within you praying perfect prayers,
    I Am One in purpose with Theirs.

I Am God, The Holy Spirit within,
    Life-Giver, this Revival to begin.
By Me you can know Jesus is Lord,
    I Am Author of the Inspired Word.

I Am One with The Father and Son,
    The battle fought is already won.
The people of the earth need Revival,
    Are ready to go beyond survival.

The Book of Acts describes the way we ran
    To establish the Church Jesus began.
I Am The Holy Spirit, God's voice you hear
    Be ready to hear Me. Do not fear.

                A.M.T., June 28, 1999

1 Corinthians 12:3

PENTECOST NOW

Here I AM, flesh and blood I stand!
    See My side, My love-scarred hand.
Here, I see your joy, take My peace,
    Now you can forgive and release.

As I was sent by Our Father, so are you.
    Receive My Spirit, be made new.
I've prayed for others who will hear
    About Me from you, in holy fear.

Throw out your fishwork nets;
    Worldly people filled with regrets
Want to be, in your nets caught,
    To hear My word, by Me be taught.

You will know Me all the more,
    See abundance as never before.
You will call for help from partners
    My Christians, your neighbors.

In extravagant love, I make you one,
    Taking part in harvest I have won
By My cross, as God's power and wisdom
    Now Risen King of His Kingdom .

A.M.T., May 24, 1999

John 20:19-23; John 17: 17-22;
1 Corinthians 1:22-25

GETHSEMANE CUP

I drank the cup of your sin and shame;
    Became sin so you could bear My Name,
Covered with My own Blood, there I stood;
    Our Father saw not your sin, but My good.

Before you know what I have done,
    Set you free, made you blameless son,
You drink your own cup of sin abomination;
    Regret and sorrow, guilt of separation.

Why carry past sins that I, Jesus, have borne?
    Repent, turn to Me to be reborn,
Forgiven, made righteous, a new creation
    In joy, peace and love, in salvation.

I AM Father who, in love, created you;
    Now, in faithful love, I create you anew
Through My Son with whom I AM well pleased;
    You are from satan's captivity released.

Now ask for Our Holy Spirit plentiful,
    So all the character of Jesus beautiful
Will begin in you on earth and bloom forever
    On earth and in heaven with Him together.

A.M.T., May 10, 1999

Matthew 26:36-42; Romans 3:23-26
John 3:16-17; 2 Corinthians 5:17; Luke 11:13

SIGNS AND WONDERS

Look clearly at My signs and wonders,
    And hear My voice that thunders.
Interpret the sign and wonder of gold
    See it as My Coming foretold.

Look at My Holy preserved Word
    And see Me. I AM LORD!
Miracles, wonders, sister and brother,
    Show you there is no other.

Look not to healing mud in eyes, or facts
    Of gold in the fish's mouth for tax,
Or the snake on Moses' staff in idolatry,
    See The Savior lifted up on The Tree.

Pray to interpret supernatural tongues,
    Miracle and wonder of heaven's songs
Given to you, My creature believers,
    Sons and daughters, heaven achievers.

You are keys given to Peter for a door
    To open for many to find the "More!"
I AM Jesus, King with Father on the throne,
    In Spirit and truth worship God alone.

Signs point to Someone, causing wonder
    Open your heart to Me and ponder.
Say My Word boldly, send light and healing,
    Holy Spirit power, My love revealing.

                      A.M.T., March 1999

Psalm 29; John 3:14
Matthew 17:24-27; Acts 4:29-31

THE FATHER'S LOVE

My Son raised up, lifts you above
    To know My eternal plan of love.
That by Our Spirit, you would be
    A valued member of Our Family.

I Am Father God, there is no other,
    Jesus purchased you as His brother
I Am Father to you who believe Him,
    Lord and Savior, receiving Him.

Your body a temple, space within for Me
    Your spirit, My breath from eternity.
Born again, you will know your worth,
    Ask for My Spirit and "new birth."

Do not wait or hesitate, I Am at your gate!
    Open the door, in surprise to realize
You will know love when you've know mine
    Filling you, overflowing light to shine.

My love for you flows without reservation
    In joyful Resurrection celebration!
As you follow Me gladly in freedom's way,
    Receiving My love and giving it away.

A.M.T., April 9, 1999

John 3: 1-17; 8:36; 10:29; 14:23

CHOSEN AND SENT

I have called you, chosen and sent.
    You heard and quickly went.
Now wait for power from on high,
    My Second Coming is nigh.

I call to you "Let all else go!
    Jump deep into The River flow
From My throne, out heaven's door
    To bring to My people More!"

Each of you are My "riverbed stone"
    Formed in River from My Throne,
Living Water from My crucified side
    Has now become a flood tide.

You, My smooth stones, living witness
    Skimmed by Me; ripples, splashes
Over My people yet to come, to sense
    By The Spirit, Our Father, My presence.

Called, sent, ruined and ready,
    O God, I say, "Here I am, send me."
In Your Love, by Your Spirit, I'll tell them
    You are here to save, not to condemn.

A.M.T., May 17, 1999

Isaiah 6:1-8; John 3:16-17;
Revelation 22:1-7

EPHESIAN'S PRAISE

He chose us in His good will, His pleasure
    To make us His possession, His treasure.
O grasp how high, how deep, wide and long
    Is the love of Him to whom we belong.

To make us holy sons, He gave us His Son!
    A "divine exchange" and we then won
Life eternal through His Blood of grace
    Able to look at His Glorious Face!

Father, "Abba!" You, I adore! Giving more
    Than immeasurably imagined or asked for,
The strength and power of Your Spirit Holy.
    Forever my Lord, Jesus, I give You glory!

A.M.T., March 9, 1999

Ephesians 1 & 3

GOD IS LIFE

See My Life reflected in a growing thing
    Tend your garden, hear the birds sing.
I created, in love, the earth and you,
    Said "it is good" and planned too.

You are mortal, pilgrim traveling through;
    I, Jesus, took on satan and death for you.
Your life in Me begins not in rebirth,
    Born of the Spirit, while still on earth.

I teach and have parables for you now;
    I want you to know and understand how
I love you, desire you to know My ways:
    Redeeming, forgiving your yesterdays.

My plan is for you eternity, infinity,
    My precious child, of limited ability.
My good plan beyond imagination
    My goal is your unending salvation.

Be at peace, favored child of mine,
    I want you to be in My family divine.
I will pursue you, joyful love abiding,
    Waiting, beloved, for your deciding.

A.M.T., June 1999

John 3:16

WHO AM I?

I, God, created you in your mother's womb,
    Wrapped you in skin, color of My choice.
Made a space within for Me to reside, and
    Gave you bones so you could stand.

I, Jesus, Deliverer, there at your birth
    Set you free before your life on earth.
Yes, I died for you, yet I live as King
    Of Kingdom prepared for your choosing.

I Am the Truth, the Life, and the Way
    To our Father whose love is here to stay.
There is more, you will find, as you pursue
    Me, God of the Universe, who loves you.

O God, I hear You at the door of my heart,
    I receive You and Your Spirit. Never depart!
I accept the glorious freedom You've won,
    I choose step-by-step the way of Your Son.

Now, I see You have blessed me in the past,
    Given mercy and grace in a plan to last.
The best gift is Your presence. I believe,
    Worship You and Your word I receive.

A.M.T., June 1999

Psalm 139:13-18; John 8:36
Revelation 3:20; 7:2-17

GARDENS

In Eden's Garden You walked with us
    In the cool of the day
And clothed us, Yourself,
    When we fell away.

In Gethsemane Garden You bled,
    With tears of love for us.
Beside the Garden Tomb,
    You walked victorious!

You stood before Mary
    And called her name.
And, now, You have
    Called mine the same!

Ever will I meet You
    To converse in prayer;
In the Garden You choose,
    I will be there.

A.M.T., April 1999

Genesis 3:8; Luke 22:44
Matthew 26:36-46; John 20:16
Song of Songs 8:13

II
INTERCESSION:

THERE IS NO OTHER

JESUS PRAYING

PRODIGAL RETURN

CRIES & TEARS

ALIEN, STRANGER, PILGRIM

THIS BLESSED TASK

ROYAL PRIESTHOOD

INTERCESSION FOR A CITY

ACTS TODAY

I READ THE NEWSPAPER

PEDESTRIAN

THERE IS NO OTHER

I AM the Lord, there is no other,
    My Son is Savior, there is no other.
Life is a pilgrimage, a choice, a test
    For you to choose what is best.

I give each of you an opportunity
    To choose Me and Life for eternity.
Do you trust My love for each?
    Are you sure that I reach and teach?

Come to Me, find Me whom you seek,
    Ask in faith when you pray for the weak,
Have no shame that I use affliction to tame
    My sons for whom I desire My Name.

I AM God of Abraham, Isaac and Israel
    With a mighty plan to save you from hell.
Put your trust in Me and My Son as well
    Worship in Spirit & Truth; do not rebel.

O God, I believe! Help my unbelief!
    I repent, turn to You in love, and relief,
To realize Your Love and pleasure
    In seeing our faith as Your treasure.

You had a plan that included all of us,
    For the sacrifice of Your Son, Jesus.
For Your perfect will on earth, I look above;
    Your plan includes me and those I love.

                        A.M.T., April 1999
Isaiah 45:5,22; John 19:30; 20:16;
Hebrews 11:39-40

JESUS PRAYING

Father, I stand before You, Your Son,
    God, High Priest, yet human One,
Pain forgotten, My heart in compassion
    For this child of My suffering passion.

I ask You, Father, for this need for this son,
    This daughter beloved I have won.
Pour out Your Spirit of Truth and conviction
    So this child of mine, from sin will run.

Dear Father, awesome love is Your glory,
    Your mercy, gives justice solid victory.
Forgive and heal, in trust I kneel, and ask.
    In Your love, let this one bask.

Our Life-Giver Spirit, Word in love attention
    Is gift waiting; what will get their attention?
O Father may they be one with Me and know
    Your love for us is in abundant flow.

Father, My heart breaks anew for this one,
    Give him his inheritance and let him run
In Your love pour out Your protection Spirit
    Let him have his way 'til he's sick of it.

O Lord heal his blind eyes, repeal his sentence
    He chose a pigsty, let him come to his senses.
I'll run with him as he returns and repents,
    I have readied his righteous garments.

A.M.T., March 17, 1999

John 17; 3:16; Luke 15:11-31

PRODIGAL RETURN

I come to my senses, from the pigpen I run
    To You, O God; I feel I'm no longer Your son.
I see You there, coming to greet me,
    Your arms outstretched in love and mercy!

O My Father, You're running, this wretch to meet
    With Jesus, in joy Who washes my feet!
For this robe of righteousness I wear, He bled!
    His Life, His word is my daily bread.

Father, this ring signifies that I belong
    To You, forgiven, with celebration and song!
O God, never again will I wander!
    I pray in Your Spirit for my older brother.

Who has yet to know You, and understand
    The glory of Your Spirit in Truth reprimand,
The wonder of transcendent peace, life abundant,
    Joy without limit for those repentant.

Pour out Your Spirit, to convict him in mercy.
    He doesn't deserve; neither did we.
May he and we live by Your Spirit, today
    Jesus, Loving Goodness, lighting our way.

A.M.T., May 1, 1999

Luke 15:11-32; John 14:9;
Romans 7:15-25; Galatians 5:16-25

CRIES & TEARS

On earth I talked to My Father with cries and tears
    Before Him in Majesty and awe, but my fears
Were for fellow humanity fearful of death in sin.
    I loved you then, but knew justice must win.

Son of God and human related, I, Jesus
    Prayed as one with you, for mercy for "us,"
I called disciples, brothers, to pray too
    "Father, forgive, deliver, free 'us' in You."

Our Father answered every prayer I did pray:
    "You delight in Me; You shall have your way.
I will deliver and save those sons you love.
    You're My Love, My Bread, sent from above."

I, Jesus, God's Son, took your sins, and My good,
    Became atonement sacrifice on that cross of wood,
So you could be forgiven, set free to pray with me,
    I, in you and you in Me, High Priest for eternity.

Our Father and I give you Our Spirit to relate
    As believers who receive Me and communicate
With love and praise to join My intercession,
    Adoring Our Father who loves us in compassion.

A.M.T., June 22, 1999

Hebrews 5:7-10; 4:15-17
John 17; Psalm 37:4

ALIEN, STRANGER, PILGRIM

O God, I am alien, stranger, pilgrim on earth.
    Your Father's blessing followed my new birth.
In faith we follow You as ancients before us,
    Heaven is opened because of Lord Jesus.

O Father, Your Spirit and love I receive,
    In You and Your plan of good, I believe.
I pray with Jesus as one of His sheep,
    Hear His voice, swim in Your River deep.

In Him we are made righteous, joyful and free
    Because of His sacrifice on that tree.
We are surrounded by a cloud of witnesses
    Faithful to You, God of fulfilled promises.

Eyes fixed on Jesus in faith and hope, seeing
    Heavenly Jerusalem; You Living God waiting.
We intercede in faith for those to come,
    Knowing Your plan for us in Your Kingdom.

A.M.T., Dec. 29, 1999

1 Kings 19:9-18; Hebrews 11 & 12
John 17

THIS BLESSED TASK

Father, You love me, that's why I ask
    For grace to do this blessed task
Of being wife to this man you've given,
    Steward of our children from heaven.

Father, Creator, Source of Life,
    Loving us in a world of sin and strife,
Forming us to be Bride and Wife
    Of Your Son for eternity Life!

O God, I look at springtime beauty,
    In children I see reflected Your glory.
I see in my neighbor and my own aging face
    Lines of experience, expressions of grace.

Thanks and praise rise from within myself,
    Blessings, memories, on mind's treasure shelf
And I wonder, "Is this reflected beauty we see,
    In fullness of new heaven and earth, to be?"

I wait in hope with joy in my heart
    To see You in fullness; now I know in part
To be known by You, in completed life's story,
    To know You fully, in Your glory!

A. M.T., May 27, 1999

John 3:16; 1 John 3:1, 4:16;
Hebrews 2:9-18, 4:9-16; Romans 14:17
1 Corinthians 13:12

ROYAL PRIESTHOOD

My greatest compassion is for this nation
    Of people who don't know My gift of salvation.
I AM High Priest interceding the Day before
    I come as just Judge, or merciful Savior.

I called & chose you, My Church, Royal Priesthood,
    Holy, suffering servants, purchased by My Blood
To proclaim the call of Our Father of Might
    "Come out of darkness into My marvelous light."

My living stones, exiled in shame, suffering & pain,
    Compassionate love has been your gain.
Your sin erased, your death raised, you understood
    The same is for each in your neighborhood.

I Am Shepherd saying "This is the way, walk in it."
    You have been prepared by My Holy Spirit.
Do not falter, do not wait or hesitate,
    But open the door. I Am at the gate!

I AM the King of Glory, holiness and light;
    You, My living stones, My temple, My earthly might.
Suffer injustice, endure hardship, love by my grace
    Know I Am with you; stay in My loving embrace.

A.M. T., Spring 1999

1 Peter 2:4-6; Psalm 24:7-10
Isaiah 30:21

INTERCESSION
FOR A CITY

By myself I cannot say a thing that's wise.
    I see you with God's compassionate eyes
And realize that for you Jesus' blood did flow.
    By The Spirit, hands raised, I pray thus so:

"Lord Jesus, a bruised reed You did not break
    For each person, Your heart does ache.
Through Your Spirit, You bring life and love,
    To each created by Our Father above.

"O Lord God of love, bless each one in need.
    For these brothers and sisters I intercede.
Forgiven sinner I am, weak and unworthy
    But I respond to speak with Your authority.

"Father in heaven, praise to Your Holy Name,
    Desire for Kingdom living, is Your aim.
Jesus, daily Bread, Deliverer, give Life.
    Holy Spirit, inspire repentance for strife.

"Jesus, Your cross has won us forgiveness,
    Enabling us to change, forgive and bless.
Now, I pray, Sovereign, Risen Lord, have pity,
    And deliver from the evil one, this City.

"Oh Lord, we are many types of many races.
    Make us one by Your generous graces.
Forgive us in the city and surrounding counties,
    And pour out Your blessings and bounties."

A.M.T., March 18, 1999

Matthew 12:20
2 Corinthians 1:3-5; Acts 10:34

ACTS TODAY

O God from the mockery I see, I flee
    To You, for refuge in Your victory.
Is persecution, this dispersal a rehearsal
    For disaster to come?

May my way and my thoughts today,
    And the last thought, the word I say
Be "In You, O God, I believe,"
    In the hour this earth I leave.

I Am Lord, hearing you whom I created.
    Son Jesus died for you and We waited,
Saved your place in Our family 'til you came
    To Us to receive His Spirit and Name.

Come blessed brother, sister, also friend;
    Our Kingdom come, for you does not end,
Whether on earth you leave or stay,
    Walk in freedom and Joy as I Am your way.

                      A.M.T., May 5, 1999

John 3:16; Acts 7:59-8:1
Matthew 25:34

I READ THE NEWSPAPER

I read the newspaper about war and cloning,
    Sin abounding, people disowning
Their own, and I cry to God for relief,
    I know Jesus, on the Cross, bore this grief.

He gave the answer then, and gives it now:
    "Come to Me," you burdened, weary, see how
The Son of God is The Way, The Life, The Truth,
    The One to save the old and youth.

My daughter, The Father and I, One in heart,
    With love for you never to depart,
Created your free will, a blessing, not a curse,
    In likeness of the One King of the Universe.

Each of you have Our gift in glorious freedom
    To repent, & run to Father of the Kingdom
Now, My daughter, in the Name of My Son,
    Ask for The Holy Spirit for each one.

The Spirit of wisdom sent is Our own,
    To contrast righteousness and sin sown
Only By The Spirit can each one repent to know
    My Son, Jesus, is the only Way to go.

A.M.T., June 14, 1999

Genesis 1:26-27
John 14:6-10; 16:7-11

PEDESTRIAN

I see drivers' faces as I wait to step off the curb
    We want to cross the street, not traffic disturb;
Three red cars, a taxicab, and a school bus,
    No one waves, smiles or waits for us.

Like tennis match spectators, our heads turn
    Right to left, and back again. We'll get sunburn!
Then suddenly I wake up and remember to pray
    Blessings over the unsmiling drivers in the way.

Hurrying people, no doubt with duties galore;
    Has any one prayed for them before?
These precious people, this drive-by community,
    Racing to go somewhere, each with a story.

I ask God, our Father to tell me how to begin
    To pray by The Holy Spirit within
And I realize that Jesus for each one died
    And lives for each one to be sanctified.

I "prayer walk." Now I "prayer stand," waiting
    Asking for each today, deliverance and blessing,
Joy, peace and holiness, while I wonder happily
    If a waiting pedestrian once prayed for me?

                          A.M.T., June 14, 1999

John 15:15-17; Philippians 4:6
1 Peter 3:12

III
WITNESSES

EACH WITH A STORY

ENOCH

FAITH SEES HOPE

MARY

SIMEON & ANNA

NICODEMUS

GRANDMOTHER GRACE

PROPHETS

FREEDOM SONG

OUT OF THE BOX

NOW IS THE DAY

SONS OF GOD ARISE

THESE TWO COMMANDMENTS

WORSHIP MEETING PLAN

TRAVELING SONG

WONDERFUL LORD

SERVANT MESSENGERS

EACH WITH A STORY

We come, each with a story.
    Don't fit into a category,
Amateurs who come in love,
    Each with a gift from above.

We rejoice in the God of Israel,
    Who sets us free, makes us well,
Righteous servants serve without fear,
    In His holiness, one more year.

Jesus, Your mercy is tender.
    Covenant of peace You remember.
Holy Spirit, Life-Giver to the fragile,
    Brings light joy to the less agile.

A.M.T., Jan. 31, 1999

"Praise be to the Lord, the God of Israel, because He has come and has redeemed His people. He has raised up a horn of salvation for us . . salvation from our enemies . . . . to show mercy to our fathers and to remember His holy Covenant . . . to rescue us from the hand of our enemies, and to enable us to serve Him without fear in holiness and righteousness before Him all our days."
(Luke 1:68-75 - Zechariah's Song)

ENOCH

Enoch and God took a walk,
    Faithful friends, eager to talk.
One day they walked so far away
    God said, "My home is closer,
    Come in and stay."

O God, my Shepherd Lord, You speak,
    I listen for Your voice and seek
To walk and talk with You day by day
    Until I, too, hear You say,

"My home is closer, come in and stay."

A.M.T., April 1999

Genesis 5:18-24
Hebrews 11:5
Jude 14

FAITH SEES HOPE
Hebrews 11

Noah, blameless by faith, the ark built,
    Abraham had righteousness, not guilt.
Sarah's laughter turned to joy
    As she bore Isaac, Abraham's boy.

From Abraham came people of faith, more
    Than stars in sky, or sand on seashore,
Persons, living by faith when they died
    Went to God-of-the-Promise to reside.

Aliens and strangers on earth, they lived in hope
    Of heavenly home, therefore could cope
With persecution, mistreatment and sword
    Because hope was in our Faithful Lord.

Our Father, God, had a plan that included us;
    By His Spirit to reveal to each of us, Jesus.
At Transfiguration, Moses and Elijah did prove
    That all are alive in Him who does not move.

There is only one goal, one plan in this life
    This pilgrimage that is so filled with strife:
To choose to turn to God, to repent;
    To know His love by One Whom He sent.

A.M.T., May 3, 1999

Genesis 6:9; Genesis 18
Hebrews 11; Luke 9:28-36; John 17:3; Jeremiah 29:11

MARY

The God of Abraham, Isaac and Israel,
    Sent to virgin Mary His main Angel.
The Holy Spirit filled her when he spoke,
    No person or family did she invoke.

She said her "yes" to God on earth,
    To the Son of God, she gave birth,
Faithful always; there at Pentecost,
    Has a mother's heart for the lost.

She is sent from God as messenger,
    Not for the Saved to look at her.
She is saying, "To Him, listen!"
    Open your eyes, see the vision.

Eyes of faith see Jesus to ask Him in;
    Repent, turn, away from your sin.
Know His own Word, Him as Savior
    Who comes on the clouds as Victor!

Our Father, God of Might and Majesty
    Has for us a blessing of immensity
To empower us with Holy Spirit grace
    To see, with Mary, His Son's face.

A.M.T., April 1999

Luke 1:26-38; Acts 1:14;
Matthew 24:30; John 19:25

SIMEON & ANNA

Simeon, called by the Spirit to the temple
    Never realized he was the example
To the elderly; that recognizing Jesus
    Makes old age a time glorious!

Anna, there in the temple with Simeon
    Knew God's work when she saw it on
Her worship journey of fasting and prayer,
    Hurrying to tell others of Jesus there.

Simeon, respected elder at the gate,
    No longer striving to compete or imitate;
Ready to go, able to know Spirit revelation,
    Found Jesus, God's Son, our salvation.

Sovereign God, for us Child born, Son given,
    Prince of Peace! God of Heaven!
Wonderful! Counselor! Light of the nations
    Brings righteousness, Justice, our salvation!

Dismiss me, Lord, I'm ready to leave
    You are Faithful Promisor, whom I believe.
You formed me in my mother's womb,
    Planned my days, my rising from the tomb.

By Your Cross, death for believers is a door
    Open to heaven where there is "More!"
By Your Spirit, Jesus, "first of many others,"
    We know we are Your sisters and brothers.

                      A.M.T., April 1999

Luke 2:25-38; 10:23-24

NICODEMUS

Nicodemus, like a lot of us,
    Secretly wanted to know Jesus
Who said you must be "born again" to come
    By The Holy Spirit into God's Kingdom.

Not to perish in your sins, for condemnation,
    But for receiving eternal salvation.
This by love of The Father Who sent His Son,
    Atonement sacrifice lifted up, salvation won.

Nicodemus believed, spoke to other Pharisees,
    Brought myrrh & aloes to help Arimathea's
Joseph laid the body of Jesus to rest in the tomb
    Not perceiving this was Resurrection womb!

Early in the morning, on the first day of the week
    Mary Magdalene came to weep, tomb to seek.
She saw it was empty, Jesus alive and speaking!
    He is Life to His disciples, us, the believing.

A.M.T., April 12, 1999

John 3: 1-21; 7:50-52; 19:38-42
John 20: 29-31

GRANDMOTHER GRACE

O Lord, I sit here, amazed, in hope,
    In awe of You, realizing the scope
Of Your plan for Life on earth
    And in eternity, with this birth.

My God and Father, still Creator
    As once, is now, and are forever,
There is no life from You apart,
    Creating out of love in Your heart.

This child, in Your image created to be,
    Your son for all eternity!
O my God, today everything is new,
    Seeing with my eyes what You do!

Jesus, God's Lamb, slain before this born son;
    Through You saved, is another generation
Of family, each given the Kingdom choice.
    Give me, for him, Your Spirit and voice.

Dear Lois, My daughter, I answer your prayer,
    Grandson, Timothy, give you for loving care.
Receive My love, My Spirit to say, to know,
    To help him, in grace and wisdom, grow.

A.M.T., June 9, 1999

Psalm 127:3; 2 Timothy 1:5
Psalm 139

PROPHETS

Prophets thrown into a man-made well,
    Man trying to make heaven or hell.
O Lord, posthumous recognition is fine
    Obedient. I speak Your words in mine.

O Lord You hear me, afflicted, crying out,
    Answer my praise, lift me up with a shout
To sit among Your princes in heavenly praise,
    To hear Your Words of love that raise.

Father, Creator, Maker of the Universe,
    Jesus, Son, Savior, Who gives me verse,
Holy Spirit within, joy and worship victorious,
    I praise and adore You, Lord Glorious!

My daughter, My son, you are My letter,
    My words written on your heart better
Than on stone tablets as law to kill;
    Holy Spirit words to give life, to fulfill.

I will give you My words of weight,
    Apart from Me, you can't get it straight
My words are all there, but today for the wise
    I AM sending My letter for accepting eyes.

A.M.T., May 29, 1999

Jeremiah 38:9; Psalm 113; Matthew 10:40-42
Acts 2:17; 2 Corinthians 3:3; 1 Thessalonians 5:19-20

FREEDOM SONG

Now I am old and I'll wear purple,
Sing of my love of God and people.
No longer image concerns,
No more points to earn.

>Refrain: Lord, I seek Your face
>   At the end of the race.

With joyful hope I proclaim
The coming of my Lord, His aim
To take me home to His Kingdom;
Lord, in response, I will come.

Father, You hear my every prayer
Through Jesus, my Lord, Your heir.
I worship You in Spirit and truth,
You've forgiven the sins of my youth.

Cleansed by the blood of Jesus Cross
I count my achievements as dross.
Pilgrimage pain forgotten, now pure love
With You, in fullness of the Spirit above.

My handicap has aged me into wisdom,
Awaiting with joy Your Kingdom
Persecuted, disdained, You understand us,
Broken, I began to know You, Jesus.

God of merciful love, You took our death
And forgave us with every breath.
I love You Lord, for You only is there room
In my heart for You, Church's Bridegroom.

A.M.T., September 12, 1998

OUT OF THE BOX

Come out of the box that has no locks;
    I, Jesus, have set you free to follow me
To others who in My word reside
    And, also remain by My side.

I have prepared you in advance,
    Nothing has been left to chance,
For the work of harvest has begun,
    To reap fruit planned by Me, Son.

I AM Son, and son are you.
    My Church, My Bride, I live for you.
Garments prepared of rightness bright,
    Sons revealed to show My might.

All creation groans in waiting
    For sons of God revealed, relating
To one another in rightness and peace
    Sons of Our Father, in Spirit release.

More than conquerors in You who loves us,
    We proclaim You, Our Lord Jesus.
You have loved us first and before
    So we can tell others there is "More!"

A.M.T., May 24, 1999

John 4:34-38; 8:36;
Romans 8:14-22, 37

NOW IS THE DAY

Now is the day of God's favor and salvation.
    We wait in holy anticipation,
Endure in loving joy our day,
    Put no stumbling block in anyone's way.

O Lord, we're a group you've readied,
    Aging people You've called and steadied,
Blessed beyond our natural skill,
    Hard workers, now show us Your will.

We've lived a long life; "been there, done that,"
    Know what counts, for what "to go to bat,
Know God is the goal; trivia is "oh whatever."
    We're close to lasting life more than ever.

I AM calling you, elders, My friends,
    Simeon's and Anna's, as this century ends.
You are a formidable force of life,
    Spirit-filled, fearless, facing strife.

You are My born-again "elders at the gate"
    Set free by My Son, it's not too late
To speak by Holy Spirit faith and be heard
    You are My letter, My living word.

A.M.T., June 14, 1999

Hebrews 3:13-15; Proverbs 31:23
Luke 2:25-38; 2 Corinthians 3:3

SONS OF GOD, ARISE!

Followers of My Son, Jesus: Arise!
    Precious young, fragile old, to shame the wise.
Stand up in My righteousness, abhor the wrong,
    Blend your voices with the heavenly song.

My Son, Jesus is Lord, there is no other.
    In His Name you are saved, sister and brother.
He is One with Me, Father, Spirit and Truth,
    Choose! Give Him the strength of your youth.

My old ones, at the end of your pilgrimage,
    Accept with joy your sufferings of age,
Share your faith as you walk your last,
    Your days before glory are going fast.

As a fetus grown you know I wipe away tears,
    Lead you, victorious, through many fears.
Now growing old with fire-tried faith of gold,
    Refuse baby tissue! Be brave and bold.

My people, by My Spirit, fearless and strong,
    Whether your life is short or long,
Live your precious life emboldened by My
    Holy Spirit to live, ready to die.

I AM Jesus. Hear My call. Come to Me,
    My workmanship, you are gloriously free.
Sons of God, revealed to live and shine
    As witnesses to Love, reflecting Mine.

                                A.M.T.

1 Corinthians 1:27; Hebrews 11
Ephesians 2:10; John 14:19;
Romans 8:19; Colossians 2:6-8

THESE TWO COMMANDMENTS

Jesus, knowing Himself as Son much loved
    Was able to worship Our Father above
And as perfect man, could love others,
    Proclaiming to be "first of many others."

He revered God's power and immensity,
    His Holy Spirit sent in generosity,
He responded with praise and worship
    In the joy of perfect Sonship.

Loving The Father, heart, mind & soul;
    Beloved Himself, He loved us whole.
Firstborn Son, "first" meaning "before"
    Redeemed us to beloved neighbor.

Jesus, Lord, I pray; show me how
    To respond in worship, to bow,
Know myself beloved, so I can love too
    Others bought with Blood by You.

Holy Spirit, Life-giver let me realize
    That I'm God's beloved and recognize
What You have done for me and others too.
    O God You are Love; may I reflect You.

                      A.M.T., April 9, 1999

Matthew 22:37-40

WORSHIP MEETING PLAN

Today I repent, remembering willful insists,
    Opportunity, divine appointments missed!
I ask the Lord for sin's bad fruit deliverance:
    Confusion, fears, timidity in circumstance.

Forgiven, delivered, I plan in His mercy
    Running to my Lord Jesus, in joy, thirsty
For the Living Holy Spirit, the flowing Water
    From the Throne of God, Our Father!

Memory from "Treasure Shelf" in my mind:
    Shopping with kids saying firmly but kind,
"Keep your eyes on me, or I'll wander and when
    You look, I'll be lost to you my children."

The Lord speaks now, through Hebrews 12:2
    "Keep your eyes on Me, your day to be new.
I Am Author, Finisher of your faith, and today
    In My care, let Me show you Love's Way."

So today as God's beloved child I'm planning
    Worship songs for those He is sending.
Through Jesus, Lord, by Holy Spirit inspiration
    I prepare in joyful praise and anticipation.

A.M.T., June 17, 1999

Hebrews 12:2; Romans 8:26-27
Galatians 4:6; John 17:6; Revelation 22:1

TRAVELING SONG

Each blade of grass, every leafy tree and I
Proclaim Your beauty as we drive by.
Beautiful sunset reflects Your glory.
Sky in blue shine or stormy
Shows Your strength and might.
You are Lord of my day and night.

Clouds of light, or dark clouds of sorrow,
With You I anticipate tomorrow.
Conqueror, over comer in You am I
Born anew, in answer to my cry.
Your Church, joyous Bride are we
Reflecting Your light so happily.

Joy, praise and worship
Exalting Your Name,
Ever and ever, You we proclaim.

A.M.T., September 12, 1998

WONDERFUL LORD

Creator, Savior, Comforter, Majesty,
    Complete, Holy, yet creating me!
Compassionate, gracious, loving us,
    Seeing us sinners, sending Jesus.

O Lord, You love all You have made.
    Father, You come to our aid.
Jesus, the Way, the Light, and the Truth,
    On Your cross forgive sins of youth.

O God of all, we are sons rebellious,
    Yet in Your love, You sent Son Jesus.
In thanks and praise and worship I bow;
    In freedom, forgiven, life begins now.

In The Holy Spirit I read my Concordance
    I praise, I worship, I sing, I dance.
Wonderful Lord! In You I rejoice,
    Pursuing Your word, Your voice!

                A.M.T., March 8, 1999

Psalm 145:13; John 1:4,14:6
Romans 3:23-25; Psalm 149:1-5

SERVANT MESSENGERS

My Church, each of you, earthly presence,
    Of Our love, joy, Our very essence.
By Our Holy Spirit you walk among
    People of the world with talk and song.

Living water within from My side of sacrifice,
    Convicts the sinner, humbles the wise.
Consider your presence as "prayer walking"
    I Am sending you as My Truth talking.

Speak My words of reality and salvation;
    Darkness must leave before celebration.
Condemned "prince of the world" depraved.
    By Me, JESUS, only, are you saved.

The Holy Spirit shows, convicts the sinner
    Repenting, we turn to Jesus, The Winner
To know the Father's peace and love
    Asking for abundant Life from above.

A.M.T., April 29, 1999

John 13:16-20; 16:7-11

IV
HEALING

I NEED HEALING

BROKEN TEMPLE

HOLD OUT YOUR HAND

THAT'S WHY I ASK

THORN IN MY SIDE

SUPPORT IS A STEPPING STONE

GOD'S EMBRACE

THE WORD AMONG US

SOVEREIGN LOVE WINS

MY UNCLE WAS HEALED

ISAAC'S WOOD

I TOUCHED HIM

THESE ARE MY PEOPLE

BEYOND HEALING

I NEED HEALING

I need healing you see, and say,
    And over me you do pray.
God touches me again and again
    But outwardly, I look the same.

Living water of God bubbles up and flows.
    Healing shines out where only God knows.
My life is new! Pray some more!
    My God-time in a chair, yours on the floor.

I see visions of heaven where I dance.
    My healing I see in advance.
My laughter begins now on earth
    In my Lord, Jesus all is of worth.

With me in valley of suffering and death,
    His rod, His staff; His very breath.
His presence is comfort, Himself mercy,
    As He disciples me toward eternity.

Joy fills my soul at the end of life's race
    Please know I experience this grace,
Let us rejoice in our Father's good plan
    By The Holy Spirit, this joy began.

A.M.T., February 1999

Psalm 23; Romans 8:18
Hebrews 11

BROKEN TEMPLE

I am a broken temple
    Born to be an example.
God completes what He does start.
    Here on earth we see in part.

I am a wounded clay pot,
    Pleasing to some I am not.
Father God plans in me
    To show the wise, eternity.

My healing complete will come
    On entering His Kingdom.
Now on earth, He in me does shine,
    A wineskin for His new wine.

I rejoice in Your love, Jesus, Lord.
    My dancing heart hears Your Word.
I love You my God, my heart's desire,
    Holy Spirit within, an eternal fire.

A.M.T., Feb. 1999

Isaiah 45:9; 1 Corinthians 2:9

HOLD OUT YOUR HAND

He said, "hold out your hand," and there I stood,
    Hiding the withered, holding out the good.
As I matured, I dropped that deceptive lie
    And no longer did He pass me by.

I walk in the valley, aged and weak;
    In Him my courage; Him only I seek.
His rod, His staff, His presence my strength,
    My life now His, my journey His length.

With age, wrinkles come to my mortal body,
    Discomforts too, borne less gladly;
My life in Glory Land is closer than before,
    Yet into my elation comes the Tempter.

"Ha! Lazarus! Dying you are, not healed!
    Hey Lazarus, was your rising repealed?"
"No! Healing, a sign of eternal life, new wine
    Of the Holy Spirit, is mine as believer."

I rejoice in petitions filled with thanksgiving;
    To Jesus, Savior, Miracle Worker, living!
To You Father, Son and Spirit I sing praise,
    By Your grace I follow Your ways.

A.M.T., February 1999

John 11:1-44
Philippians 4:4-7

THAT'S WHY I ASK

Father, in Your immense love I bask;
    That's why, in need, I ask
You to bless me while I'm ill.
    Give the doctor Your healing skill.

Father, You love me, so I implore
    In trust of You for this favor
For this friend, for that neighbor.
    Heal them too, bless their doctor.

Jesus, Lord, High Priest interceding,
    In Your Holy Word I'm reading
Of The Father's love when You He sent
    To give Life to us earthly transient.

Pilgrims with inherited mortality,
    We believe, receive in You, eternity;
On earth, in Your Spirit, begin to be wise,
    Knowing Your love in sacrifice!

My children, My daughters and sons,
    In Jesus, resurrected, My suffering ones,
You have courage, victory, Sabbath rest.
    Your life grows in His character blest.

I, Jesus, forgive, free you, send you as seed
    To dwell in peace among people in need
As children of Our Father, faithful in strife,
    Righteous in joy-Spirit of My life.

A.M.T., May 26, 1999

John 3:16; 1 John 3:1, 4:16
Hebrews 2:9-18, 4:9-16; Romans 14:17

THORN IN MY SIDE

My thorn is there and I have prayed
    It is a fact, acceptance now made.
Now the Lord is showing me why
    And how to live before I die.

Jacob, now Israel, never walked the same,
    After meeting the Lord of wrestling fame.
Paul, sick or well, whether rich or poor,
    Thorn and all, moved on to "More!"

Oh, Lord take this up, let it be done.
    Not my will but Yours, for Kingdom.
I limp, I move, the thorn to remind
    Me of You; I'm not left behind.

Jesus, yesterday and today, still heals
    Where weakness is, His strength reveals.
Lord, I turn my eyes to Your wonderful face,
    In boundless love, You give Your grace.

In my heart, a praise and worship song,
    To You, Lord and Bridegroom, I belong
My joy overflowing is seen by others,
    I'm a witness to sisters and brothers.

A.M.T., March 18, 1999

2 Corinthians 12:7-10; Hebrews 13:8
John 3:29; Genesis 32:22-32

SUPPORT IS A STEPPING STONE

Support is a stepping stone, repentance a door;
    Belief is the key, opening to "More!"

Signs and wonders show me Another.
    They point to Jesus, Lord and brother!
This Brother, Jesus, with Father does wait
    For our repentance, no matter how late.

With open arms He says "Come to Me!"
    And with the Father, puts on a party!
How wonderful it is, a human to be.
    Lord Jesus, I worship You, for all eternity.

A.M.T., April 1999

Romans 10:9; Luke 15:11-32

GOD'S EMBRACE

I have My arms around you, one by one,
    My nail-scarred hands from heaven
Touching you, My light flowing through.
    No darkness can stay in you.

Raised in Resurrection, I draw you to Me,
    Pain forgot in joy of you, born for eternity.
Our Father and I reign in heaven; on earth
    I walk by Our Spirit with you of new birth.

Rejoice in The Spirit given you who desire
    To ask Our Faithful Father to send His fire;
His love to receive, and to give away,
    As you in My loving embrace stay.

A.M.T., April 1999

John 16:21

THE WORD AMONG US

I've been in exile,
    Waiting all the while
For healing in this place,
    But now near the end of the race

I call to the Lord anxiously,
    And He says, "Wait on Me,
I'll give you perfect peace.
    My love for you will never cease."

O Lord, my God, I worship You
    Who loved me first so true.
I sing to You in worship and praise.
    Love is in all Your ways.

Jesus, Your Son, is my Savior,
    Living still as "Warrior!"
By His Cross, "Conqueror!"
    By The Spirit, "Overcomer!"

Praise, thanks, loving God of "More!"
    You have opened heaven's door.
You are light, You are glorious,
    My Lord, God, Jesus.

Hallelujah, glorious Lord!
    In Genesis "The Word"
"The Word Among Us,"
    Wonderful Jesus!

                      A.M.T. 1999

John 1:1-20

SOVEREIGN LOVE WINS

Sovereign Love wins over sin troubles of earth.
    At My Word, heaven and earth new birth.
Heaven My Throne; I esteem the one contrite
    Who trembles at My Word, in fragile might.

Waiting to complete the "should" and "ought"
    Your attention on Me, Jesus, is not,
Yet when you finally listen and let go,
    I speak, and to you, My Way show.

Now, as I show you My word and witness:
    Look at My actions, and fruit, in rightness.
I healed, gave life, did miracle, sign and wonder.
    Why since have many been ill and died? Ponder.

Stephen, Paul and Cassie died at the hands of men
    Faithful, like Me martyred, truthful to the end.
Paul lived thorn in side, his weakness My strength.
    He, as did John, accepted from Me, life's length.

Each of My favored people is a witness and example
    Of the diversity of "living stones" of My temple,
Rising above the reality of trouble and dying,
    Crying out in My Spirit, in Our Father rejoicing.

A.M.T., May 6, 1999

Isaiah 66:2; John 4:23-24; 16:33
Matthew 3:9-10; Micah 7:14-20
Psalm 96

MY UNCLE WAS HEALED

My uncle was healed last Wednesday at nine,
    God took him to heaven, in journey divine.
Jesus completed what He started
    In my uncle's life, now departed.

He knew Jesus came to Him in rebirth;
    Filled with the Spirit, Paul knew his worth.
He loved God's Church and lived God's word,
    His own voice was a two-edged sword.

He was not perfect but, oh, so humbly aware
    Of God's love, he prayed in confident prayer.
By his words we knew that he never forgot;
    GOD was Sovereign and perfect, he was not!

Everything Paul said or did directed us to Jesus
    He did this in his daily life without pride or fuss
With joy in his heart and a twinkle in his eye.
    He lived knowing Jesus. He was ready to die.

I, God of holy family, say Paul is an example
    To you, also a "living stone" in My temple
Find Me in your life and My Written Word, too;
    I came to call "all" not just a few.

                      A.M.T., June 10, 1999

John 11:25-27; Acts 23:16;
Hebrews 12:2; Ephesians 1, 2, 3 ; 6:17

ISAAC'S WOOD

As Isaac carried the wood of sacrifice,
    And I provided the ram,
So, as you carry life's cross of suffering,
    Know I provide the Lamb.

My Son, Jesus, raised up, lifts you above
    Your suffering, to know My love,
My plan in Our Spirit for all eternity
    That you would be in Our family.

Your life as clay I lovingly mold,
    So your faith will be fire-tried gold.
My child I Am Lord, your loving Father,
    Bringing you to Jesus as His forever.

A.M.T., March 22, 1999

Genesis 22:6; John 16:33
Hebrews 2:11-12

I TOUCHED HIM!

O Jesus, if I could touch your garment hem,
    I know I could be done with my problem
Of pain, medical expense and disability;
    You are The One with miracle ability.

I've heard You're from the God of our fathers,
    I have followed You, not just others.
If I get close to You, I know You will heal me.
    Your love reaches out to people of frailty.

O my God! I touched You and I am healed!
    I tremble, in worship at Your love revealed.
"Go in peace, you came in faith, My daughter,
    I make you whole, I Am your Healer."

All people now hear of her miraculous release,
    Jesus still heals; He's the Prince of Peace,
Let us go to Him with faith, for our heart's desires;
    He acts in loving power for faith He admires.

A.M.T., June 26, 1999

Luke 8:43-48; Hebrews 11; 13:8

THESE ARE MY PEOPLE

These are my people, special in My eyes,
    Disabled, weak, to confound the wise.
Put them in the front so all can see
    My beloved, destined for eternity.

To family and friends, by love I Am bound,
    To these beloved lost, by Me found.
In fellowship of suffering, see My friends,
    My love for each one, never ends.

I plan for splendid crowns, permanent healing,
    Beyond death's door pilgrimage meaning
Comes clear with Me in victorious New Life;
    Erased the pain and work of earthly strife.

I Who Am show My precious children a sight
    Of My face in glory, My Wonder and Might!
These are My witnesses, My life within to shine,
    For all to see these "living stones" are Mine.

A.M.T., March 29, 1999

Matthew 11:25-26
1 Corinthians 1:23-25; Isaiah 53:3

BEYOND HEALING

I don't know how to act!
    My healing made such an impact!
Out with the cane, in with the dance!
    I'll serve when I get the chance!

O Lord, I'm lost, now healed.
    Make me a worker in your harvest field.
Grateful for love revealed I didn't deserve,
    Like Peter's mother-in-law, I'll serve.

A.M.T.

Mark 1:30-31

V
HOPE IN GOD

GOD HAS ASCENDED

FATHER'S DAY

FIRSTBORN OF MANY OTHERS

THE CORNER OF MY ROBE IS OVER YOU

HOPE SONG

WE CAME

GREATER THINGS

THE BASIC TRUTH: YOU ARE BELOVED OF GOD

GOD HAS ASCENDED

God has ascended amid joyous shouting,
    The Lord amid trumpets sounding!
Jesus, Sovereign King of Kingdom,
    The Lord Most High! Awesome!

Bow to Him Who is King of every nation,
    Bring The Sovereign Lord exaltation!
Let us all Sing to Him a Psalm of praise!
    Shouts and cries of joy to Him raise!

I AM LORD lifted up Who draws all people,
    Not just those under a Church Steeple
The humble see Me with amazed gladness,
    The arrogant proud succumb to sadness.

Come to Me and Our Father to come alive!
    There's more to life than just survive.
Believe, receive Our Spirit to be known
    By Me, Shepherd-King on the Throne.

O God, my soul finds rest in You alone,
    Salvation from You, Jesus, on the Throne.
You send Your Spirit, we are created anew.
    O Lord, I sing worship praise to You!

A.M.T., May 15, 1999

Psalm 47:5-8; Ephesians 1:18-21
John 3:14; Psalm 62:1-2; Psalm104:30-35

FATHER'S DAY

My precious children of Our Father,
    Come to Me before going any farther.
Come with faith trusting like a child,
    With new eyes, excited, past exiled.

I AM Jesus. Today, look at Me to see
    Our Father, source of goodness to be.
I Am Son, you are called and chosen
    To be revealed as His children.

By Our Spirit, reflecting goodness, light;
    Causing people to weep in delight
At heavenly sign of love on earth below:
    You revealed in virtuous fruit you show.

The new heavens and earth to be, will be
    When knowledge of God covers earth and sea
When people will weep in fear and fright,
    Repentant, longing for sin to be made right.

O Father, in repentant joy I weep and wail
    For more of Your Spirit, hope does not fail.
Lord Jesus, I worship You as beloved child in awe
    Trusting in joy; today Your kindness I saw.

A.M.T., June 19, 1999

Isaiah 11:9
Matthew 24:30-31, 36,42; Romans 3:23-26

FIRSTBORN OF MANY OTHERS

My Levites, My firstborn, set apart
    For Temple worship, desire of My heart;
Delight in Our Father, with many brothers.
    I AM the Firstborn of many others.

I AM coming on dark clouds of grace rain.
    All will see in grieving supplication pain
Over Me who is Love stronger than death.
    All to praise Our Father with every breath.

I AM the One who is, who was, who is to come,
    Fullness of the Father, King of His Kingdom.
Filled with My Spirit, you are My Bride,
    All of you thirsty, come to My side.

Lord, on me, a sinner, have mercy;
    To see You, serve You, I am not worthy.
Forgive my sins by Your grace of blood covering
    And create in me, the miracle of loving.

My Lord and my God, You I worship forever.
    Spirit and truth, Fullness of the Father,
Alpha and Omega, The Son and King,
    In the Temple with love, Your praises I sing!

A.M.T., May 20, 1999

Numbers 3:11; Luke 5:8; Romans 8:29;
Hebrews 12:27; Revelation 1:4-8
Psalm 150

THE CORNER OF MY ROBE IS OVER YOU

The corner of My robe is over you,
    My righteousness is yours too.
I, Who rescued you, now protect,
    Stay with you to make you perfect.

My perfection is holiness and love,
    Love and holiness far above
The love you have known on earth;
    You are unique and of great worth.

Washed clean in My blood, given new birth,
    You see in Me, new heaven and earth.
You are My people, My dwelling with men,
    "I Am Alpha, Omega, Beginning and End.

"The Wedding Banquet ready, you I invite,
    I have your garments clean and bright.
Come, you thirsty, drink the water of life.
    Take My Name, My Bride, becoming wife.

"Hallelujah! You reign, Lord God Almighty!
    We rejoice forever and give You glory!
Praise, honor, wisdom, thanks forever. Amen.
    Lamb, Bridegroom, Light of New Jerusalem."

A.M.T., April 1999

Psalm 93:1; Revelation 19:6-9
Revelation 21:1-6; 7:12

HOPE SONG

Disabled, now enabled to see;
Terminal, ready for eternity.
Things of the earth grow dim
In the brightness ahead in Him.

O God, I love to hear Your voice
Calling to me and I rejoice
On earth and in heaven to come,
Now and for ever in Your Kingdom.

My life of worship has begun.
I am free, Father, by Your Son.
By Your Spirit my praise is pure;
In joyous trusting worship I endure.

Eternity is now with you in my heart;
My future is sure as this world I depart
You, O Lord, await each one of us,
With Bridegroom of the Church, Jesus.

A.M.T., September 12, 1998

John 10:4; 8:36
1 Peter 1:8

WE CAME

"Go quickly into streets and alleys of town;
    bring in the poor, crippled, blind and lame."
I heard and ran, to invite and bring around
    others thirsty for God. We came,
    Our place at the table to claim.

He enabled the disabled, gave eyes to the blind,
    new names to the labeled, left no one behind.
He planned the first to be last, and the last first,
    pouring Living Water so no one would thirst.
    We came, our place at the table to claim.

He said, "I have overcome the troubles of the world."
    We heard His word, a two-edged sword hurled
that dealt with our souls to cut away fantasy and lies,
    making us new as our old life dies.
    We came, our place at the table to claim.

For me and you there was a place at the table;
    wandering and lost before, we became able
to praise God in Holy Spirit worship and love
    because of His Son Jesus' call from above.
    We came, our place at the table to claim.

Wearing righteousness purchased by Your Blood,
    we praise and worship You, Bridegroom,
    King and Lord.

A.M.T., Nov. 3, 1999

Luke 14:21
Matthew 12:20

GREATER THINGS

Greater things than I will you do.
    I could do them but I want you to
Know what it is like to be able.
    Toddler daughter, help set the table.

Little son, come, hand Me the hammer,
    I need your help this summer.
Some day with Me you will reign,
    Come work with Me to train.

Beloved children, do not fear in wonder;
    Receive My Spirit; My voice of thunder;
I've prepared a place, conquered the enemy,
    Planning joyous Life for you eternally.

Come with Me now, to see the need;
    With me, in love, let us intercede.
In loving word and action with Me present,
    Speak truth; encourage the hesitant.

Carry your own cross as I have done;
    Seek our Father's will, daughter and son,
My Resurrection Life in you to be realized,
    My plan of good for you, recognized

A.M.T., July 16, 1999

John 14:12; Revelation 3:20-21
Matthew 12:20

THE BASIC TRUTH: YOU ARE BELOVED OF GOD

GOD IS ETERNAL: " 'I AM the Alpha and the Omega' says the Lord God who is, and who was, and who is to come, the Almighty." *Revelation 1:8*

GOD IS LOVE: "God is love, and he who abides in love abides in God, and God abides in him." *1 John 4:16*

OUT OF LOVE HE CREATED US: "God created human beings in His own likeness ... male and female He created them." *Genesis 1:27*

HE SENT HIS SON: "God so loved the world that He gave His one and only Son, that whoever believes in Him may not perish but may have eternal life." *John 3:16*

HE SENT THE HOLY SPIRIT: "I will ask the Father and He will give you another Advocate to be with you for-Ever, the Spirit of Truth, He lives with you and will be in you. I will not leave you as orphans." *John 14: 16-18*

MAN IS SINFUL AND SIN HAS A PENALTY: "All have sinned and fall short of the glory of God." *Romans 3:23* "The wages of sin is death, but the free gift of God is eternal life in Christ our Lord." *Romans 6:23*

CHRIST PAID OUR PENALTY: "But God demonstrates own love for us in this: while we still were sinners, Christ died for us." *Romans 5:8*

GOD GIVES FREELY: "For it is by grace you have been saved through faith, and this is not your own doing, it is the gift of God – not by works so that no one may boast." *Ephesians 2:9*

Basic Truth: *You are Beloved of God (continued)*

LIVING SAVIOR JESUS ASKS FOR OUR RESPONSE:
"Be earnest . . . and repent. Here I AM! I stand at the door and knock. If you hear My voice and open the door, I will come in and eat with you and you with Me." *Revelation 3:20*

JESUS SAID, "ASK FOR THE HOLY SPIRIT.": "If you then, with all of your sins know how to give your children good things, how much more will your heavenly Father give the Holy Spirit to those who ask Him." *Luke 11:13*

A SIMPLE PRAYER:
     Dear God, I admit that I have sinned, and I ask You to forgive me. Lord Jesus, I open the door to my heart to receive You into my life as my Lord and as Savior Who cleanses me by Your holy blood shed on that Cross.
     Please fill me with Your Holy Spirit, so I may know You and learn how to love You, myself, and others.
     Thank You, Father, for hearing my every prayer in Jesus. Amen.

REJOICE YOU BELOVED OF GOD: "Rejoice in the Lord always. I will say it again: Rejoice! Let your good sense be evident to everybody. The Lord is near. Do not worry about anything, but in prayer and petition with gratitude, tell God all your desires. And the peace of God, which transcends all understanding will guard your hearts and your thoughts in Christ Jesus." *Philippians 4:4-7*

VI
THERE'S "MORE"!

OVERVIEW

HOMECOMING

HUMAN BEINGS ASLEEP

FORGIVEN, FORGIVING

TWO VOICES, TWO CHOICES

COME TO ME

YOU ALSO WILL LIVE

MY TREASURE

SIGNS OF LOVE

THE KING'S PROVISION

MERCY

ZACCHAEUS

OBEDIENT

PEARLS FROM PRESSURE

OVERVIEW

After the Fall, mankind migrations
    Language disassociations
Asian civilizations, Abraham's call
    Native tribes unnoticed by all.

God Himself set people in place
    Not one without gifts of grace.
He looked down and knew all
    With plan of fulfilling His call.

Rising sun, the moon, stars above
    Showed forth the Creator's love.
Buffalo herds, tall mountains seen
    Beauty here in fields green.

Hearts made to worship the Creator
    All of us chose ways other.
And God in love allowing free will
    Gave us bounty, song and skill.

Majestic God, Your divine love nature
    And power shows us as immature.
By Spirit and Truth, Jesus, Son sent
    Leads us with kindness to repent.

A.M.T., October 2002

Acts 17:26-27; Romans 1:20

HOMECOMING

I AM taking home your friend
    Do not fear, it's not the end
Of my plan for her or family
    Everlasting in eternity.

In each of you a place I made
    To be only filled by Me.
I speak to each one clearly
    Stay in trust to follow me.

Now you are on a pilgrimage
    In enemy territory of rage;
Because I have won this war,
    By shed blood I Am "door."

No one can shut the door open
    By Me, the Way to heaven.
I speak to you truth to overcome
    Fear of death to come.

O God, in faith, we hope for
    Promises we see from afar,
We know Your plan includes us
    With faith in Your Son, Jesus.

A.M.T., November 2001

Hebrews 11, Hebrews 2:15
Revelation 3:8,12

HUMAN BEINGS ASLEEP

Throughout the world we all sleep
    Examined by God in love deep.
Each one not a "human doing"
    We lie there, a "human being."

There is no Life apart from God;
    All are under the Shepherd's rod
Sinner and saint alike must sleep
    Life within to rejoice or weep.

The Holy Spirit of Life intercedes
    Knowing our deepest needs
And gives us dreams to understand
    Our life under God's hand.

The Creator loves all He has made,
    Ever ready to come to our aid,
To give loving course correction
    A new day of Resurrection.

God, Who is love, woos and waits
    For me to sleep to communicate
Because then I lie there vulnerable,
    Being quietly asleep and humble.

A.M.T. January 2002

Psalm 145:13; Job 33:14-17
Daniel 4:19-37; Joel 2:28 (Acts 2:17)
Matthew 1:20; 2:12,13,19,22; Romans 8:26

FORGIVEN, FORGIVING

I'm forgiven and forgiving
   Joyously living!
No longer opinions
   By the millions!

Judging and condemning,
   Evaluating and comparing
Are spirits that no longer rise
   Because of Jesus' sacrifice.

I remember the miracles past
   Of healings that last,
Comfort of staff and rod
   Through the valley with God.

Dancing on top of the waters
   Of affliction, with others,
Racing toward the goal,
   In Jesus becoming whole.

Oh God, I'm so glad to be old!
   Finally able to be bold
Proclaiming You from roof top,
   Words of praise never to stop!

      A.M.T., March 15, 2002

Isaiah 26:13-14; Psalm 149

TWO VOICES, TWO CHOICES

From two kingdoms, two voices,
    On earth we have two choices
One leads us to wait in hate,
    The other, in love, to relate.

In Eden the tree of good and evil,
    Opened up to serpent devil
An empty place within, for sin;
    Trouble with pride to begin.

I ratified the sin of Adam and Eve,
    Choosing self, needing reprieve,
I formed opinions and gave judgment
    About my own and other's intent.

I did good works, handed out favor,
    Covered up my inner bitter flavor,
Choosing evil, I called myself good,
    Lived by "oughts" and "shoulds."

I became free through the Son of Man
    In Jesus, Lord, my Life began.
Now I have compassion for those I see
    Like me before I knew God's mercy.

A.M.T. April 5, 2002

Genesis 2:15-16; John 8:36

COME TO ME

    I, the Lord, will inspire you to inquire
        To find the door open to you.
    I will burn away obstacles with fire
        Of my love; give you desire.

    I Am He who blots out transgression
        You discover by confession
    That I forgive for my own sake
        Sin you repent of and forsake.

    I Am Holy, bringing you to be holy
        I gave you My holy life totally
    In divine exchange by My Cross
        Dying for you and all us lost.

    Come to Me, don't be afraid
        I Am here to come to your aid.
    I know you – tough, able to rebel,
        Able to choose heaven or hell.

    I created you with a free will;
        No one can violate My plan to fill
    You with freedom & love, not hate,
        But you alone can decide your fate.

                A.M.T. April 2002

Matthew 11:28-30
Isaiah 1:18; 53;4-5; John 3:16-17

YOU ALSO WILL LIVE

For us You love, You've gone ahead
   You took Your body with you
To show us that You love us too
   And say "I have a body for you!"

Love held out with nail-scarred hand,
   Michael came to understand.
He lived, inspired by Your breath;
   Holy Spirit conquering death.

Your magnificent love set him free
   To know Our Father's generosity.
Michael received gifts of art and song
   To God's family he did belong.

Michael who loved Jesus on earth,
   Believed and accepted new birth,
Delivered from the evil one's curse
   In heaven with God of the Universe.

We will meet him there in Kingdom
   Through Jesus glorious Son
Who says "Because I live you also
   Will live" and we rejoice to know.

A.M.T. April 11, 2002

John 3:3; 3:16; 14:19
Matthew 6:13; Galatians 3:13

MY TREASURE

Each of you are My personal treasure,
    Pearl of great price beyond measure.
In love for you "I bought the farm"
    Gave my life to keep you from harm.

I gave My words so you could live,
    Gave My life so you could forgive,
Forgiven by Me, you can walk free
    On earth, and in heaven with Me.

I Am chosen Cornerstone, precious
    To our Father, majestic, glorious.
Who gave me you to be made holy,
    And I have given you My glory.

You reflect My glory as you come
    To find yourself in Me, in kingdom
Living in the Spirit in freedom
    From selfishness and rebellion.

O Lord we groan in eager expectation
    Along with all of waiting creation
For revealed Spirit-changed sons to be
    Reflections of Your good and glory.

A.M.T., April 20, 2002

Matthew 13:44-45
John 17:6,22; 1 Peter 2:6; Romans 8:19-23
Romans 8:19-23; Mark 10:18

SIGNS OF LOVE

Healed hand, a sign of love;
    A healed body, love from above,
Walking on waters of affliction with God.
    Through valley with staff and rod.

I Am God's Life and Love Word,
    Given to you by Jesus Lord
Our words are eternal for eternity,
    Bodily healing is temporary.

Many miracles you have already had
    Even when you've been bad.
My words of love pursue you still
    Giving life to you, as you will.

Choose or reject the offered "More"
    Go it alone or let Me restore
Step into my Love on a path true;
    I Am Holy Spirit loving you.

A.M.T. April 2002

John 5:8; 11:43;14:35; Psalm 23:4
Proverbs 16:9; Isaiah 30:21

THE KING'S PROVISION

Why do you stand in My provision
    And say, "I don't deserve."
You must realize you are chosen
    By Me, I Am King, to serve.

Why do you then think of the poor
    And want to run out the door
And begin to work hard again
    Without Me, what then?

Can you see I have called you,
    Given ministry to make you new,
Soaked you in oil and sweet perfume,
    Preparing you for My throne room.

By My cross you are holy for My sake
    I give you a righteous path to take.
I hold out my gold Scepter and say,
    "What is your petition today?"

As My Father heard my prayer for you,
    I hear yours, in His will, too.
Prayers as incense on His altar of grace
    Answers to come on time, in place.

A.M.T. April 30, 2002

Esther 4:9; 5:1-6; John 25:16
Psalm 23:3; Revelation 5:8

MERCY

To know My love you must take
    My mercy given from above.
Our Father sent Me for your sake,
    I AM Lamb of His love.

In love, I spat into the dirt today,
    Mixing in My own DNA
Making you new so you could see
    My cleansing, outrageous mercy.

I gave My life of my own accord.
    I AM Shepherd, as well as Lord.
Took wounds to make you whole,
    Redeemed you body and soul.

Forgiven you are able to forgive.
    Because I live, you also live,
My Holy Spirit living in you,
    Counseling, comforting too.

Know my love, My mercy given,
    I want you with Me in heaven.
For you I pour out My Spirit fire,
    Baptizing you with holy desire.

A.M.T., April 30, 2002

John 9:6; 10:14-18
John 14:15-20; Luke 3:16

ZACCHAEUS

In a tree, with hard flat eyes – Zacchaeus
   In a planned encounter with Jesus.
Jesus, on him, setting His sight,
   Said, "Zacchaeus, you're just right.

I'll come to your house to dine,
   So you'll know you can come to mine."
I, looking on, knew Zac's behavior,
   Didn't know he talked with the Savior

Who saw him with eyes of favor,
   Prophetically, beyond his behavior,
Saw him with eyes of worship shine,
   Able to trust, able to love - just fine.

Zacchaeus melted to say,
   "I'll give all fraudulent money away.
You said, 'You're worth something to me.'
   I'm honored to have you dine with me."

"No one has ever loved me true,
   Yet you say I'm worthy to you!
I quit my dirty tax collector ways
   And I see possibility in my days."

Jesus turned to me with a look of trust
   And with joy I knew I must
Trust Him to love through me,
   So I served that dinner at six-thirty.

A.M.T. April 30, 2002

Luke 19: 1-10; Psalm 66:19-20 (NIV)

OBEDIENT

You have My heart with words to say.
    Obedient, wanting My Father's way.
I Am Son and you follow joyfully;
    I have healed your eyes to see.

I came to save and not to condemn,
    It's not to be "us" and "them."
You don't have to do My mission
    You are with Me on co-mission.

You are My letter on heart of flesh,
    Written uniquely with Spirit dash,
To preach and bring others to obey
    And find Life in Me today.

When you give your testimony,
    I Am there in love and authority,
To bring to the hungry living water
    Life to become son and daughter.

O Lord, blind before I now see,
    I am a messenger You accompany.
What a privilege to be sent to represent
    One in the Spirit who is present!

A.M.T., April 30, 2002

Matthew 28:18-20; John 4:10, 39-42
Corinthians 3:2; 5:20

PEARLS FROM PRESSURE

Pressure causes the pearl to form,
    Yeast, the bread to raise.
Agony led me to long for reform
    And sin to repent and praise.

From adversity and in affliction,
    I learned to ask for direction.
God heard me and in His presence
    I learned the joy of obedience.

He said "I will test you for you to see,
    The fine person you are to be.
In Me you will be a new creation,
    See yourself with admiration.

Loving me with heart, mind and soul,
    You will become peaceful and whole,
Able to love others with strength divine
    Branch attached to the Living Vine."

O God I thank you for creating me,
    Awakening divine love in me;
In Your church bringing us Your life,
    Calling us Bride, becoming wife!

A.M.T., May 2002

Hebrews 12:1-8
Revelation 21:9

EPILOGUE:
FOR POSTERITY – MY POETRY

When I go to heaven, I leave all behind,
    Left on earth for others to find.
The treasures I collected and kept,
    The home I so often swept.

All my words written and set,
    Shared by people I never met.
Do I closely guard, hide the words,
    Jealously keep what is the Lord's?

I freely received, to freely give away,
    My love of God, and so today
I'll die to possessiveness and let go
    Of what God gave me, let it flow

Send these words on the Internet,
    Xerox them in loving intent
Put them in your card or letter;
    Make a decoupage, even better.

Be sure to note the verse and Chapter,
    Write out the Scripture if you prefer.
The Holy Spirit what the recipient needs;
    Words of God's love are His seeds.

Arlene Mary Thibault, August 21, 1999

*Matthew 10:8 "Freely you have received,
freely give."*